Noor
QUEEN OF RANTHAMBHORE

Andy Rouse & Aditya "Dicky" Singh

Contents

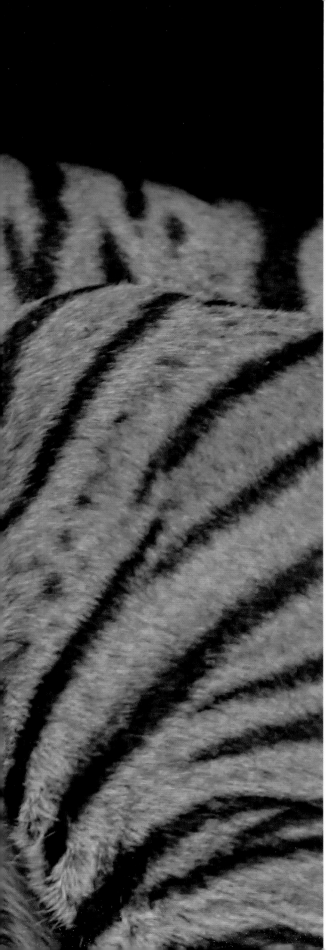

Foreword by Valmik Thapar

This book is very different from any other tiger book. In a way it is a tribute to the incredible success of Ranthambhore's tigers over the last decade. The book focusses on one tigress and her life; the amazing Noor. The pictures tell the story, the collection is brilliant and stunning; the tigers leap off the pages, bathed in dazzling light. Ranthambhore is the only place in the world that you can do an entire book on one tigress and her descendants. That is how rich it has become over time.

The turn of this century was tough and poachers wiped out nearly half of Ranthambhore's tigers, and all of Panna and Sariska's tigers. In Ranthambhore the recovery was slow and torturous. Eight of its tigers were also relocated to Sariska causing much stress to the tiger clans. In the last decade, after a huge effort by some forest officers and tiger activists, Ranthambhore evolved. New visitor-friendly rules were created that opened the secret life of tigers to both visitors and photographers. Unique protection measures were initiated that engaged local communities. Huge battles were fought behind the scenes to change the direction of the park and today, because of these measures, it is the tiger destination of the world, and this book celebrates that fact.

Aditya "Dicky" Singh and Andy Rouse capture the incredible beauty of the tiger through the story of Noor who survived this last decade and epitomises the very best of Ranthambhore's amazing tigers. I am certain that Dicky and Andy have created a book that will always be a landmark in the ever-evolving natural history of Ranthambhore's tigers.

Valmik Thapar

Valmik Thapar is India's foremost tiger expert

Introduction

Welcome to our journey. As Valmik has already said, it's not your average tiger book. It's our story, both as professional wildlife photographers and lifelong friends, of our relationship with the incredible tigress Noor. It's also a celebration of our passion for the amazing tiger habitat that is Ranthambhore National Park; a reserve that is now a conservation success story thanks to the hard work of so many dedicated people behind the scenes. In this cut-throat commercial world this book shows that two photographers with a shared commitment for conservation, and a vision for their photography, can work together to produce something truly special.

Our journey together started back in 2008 with the immortal Ranthambhore tigress Machali. Working together over a 2-month period we developed a bond and an understanding that has grown into our "family" relationship today. It was Noor that really brought us together though, as over the years this incredible tigress has opened up her lives in front of us and treated us to some incredible intimate encounters. It is these encounters that form the backbone of this book and to which we invite you to share with us.

Both of us love photographing tigers, you could say we are addicts, and we are both very good at it. It doesn't matter to either of us who has won the most awards; we enjoy sharing our photography together and bouncing ideas off each other. That is very much the philosophy of this book; you will not know who took the individual images as it doesn't matter, our time with Noor has always been a shared experience and that is the message that we want to bring from this book. Teamwork. Collaboration. United by a passion for photography, tigers and conservation. That is what defines us.

So what is so special about Noor as there are many great tigresses in Ranthambhore? It's hard to describe really, she's just the ultimate tigress for us, an incredibly ruthless killing machine one minute and a tender mother the next. There's no doubt she's a mean mamma. Really mean, sometimes scarily so. On more than one occasion her piercing stare has made both of us take our eyes back from the camera and look away. We love her all the more for this, we are drawn to her; she's our muse, we have spent every moment we can in her territory and in return she has shared incredible moments of her life with us.

Noor's territory spans Ranthambhore zones 1, 2 and part of 6; all three are tough and uncompromising places to live. Winters are freezing cold whilst the summer heat is relentless and unforgiving; everywhere you look towering bluffs dominate the skyline; dark, threatening, and unwelcoming to all comers. In this tough environment Noor has flourished, raising 3 litters to maturity, with her cubs spreading out across Ranthambhore and beyond.

In our view she's the Queen of Ranthambhore. And she knows it.

Turn the page and enter her world, the first portfolio will introduce you to Noor and the mountains that she calls home…

Noor at home

Noor's territory is dominated by immense rocky bluffs that form part of the ancient Aravalli Supergroup. As the oldest range in India and one of the oldest folded mountain ranges on the planet (the Himalayas are children by comparison), they stretch southwest from Delhi for hundreds of kilometres. An important geological fault line, the Great Boundary Fault, lies at the confluence of the Aravali and the Vindhyan systems, and runs right across Ranthambhore National Park. The huge

bluffs tower above the boulder strewn landscape below; a rich and diverse habitat that Noor has made her home.

Photographing this landscape has been a tough challenge for us. Seeing the bluffs clearly is difficult from the river valleys below as the roads are narrow, all too often we just get glimpses of their grandeur. Coupled with the unrelenting cloudless skies, we quickly realised that colour landscapes always looked

washed out. So we decided early on to use infrared (IR) modified cameras to show the harshness of the landscape and the blinding quality of the light in summer. On these pages you can see two examples of this technique, one in "colour pop" IR and one in high-contrast IR. You will see a lot of these throughout the book, it's a bold statement by us to show the environment as we see it, rather than what is "expected" in a tiger book.

The sedimentary river valleys that criss-cross Noor's territory provide a choice of water sources for her… in a good year. In a bad monsoon year however, when there isn't much rain, the water sources soon dry up and her choices become more and more limited.

Here she relaxes in the muddy waterhole by the Sultanpur forest guard post. It's shot wide to show the habitat where she lives; we have tried hard in this book to let our composition inspire you to love Ranthambhore as we do.

Across the park the excellent Forest Department ensures that these waterholes are topped up in the dry season, true conservation in action.

One of the issues we had when planning and taking the images for this book was getting a picture of Noor in the forest and mountain habitat that dominate her zones. Above you can see her hunting in the forest, just sitting waiting in the shade and being an opportunist close to a waterhole. After all everyone has to drink sometime…

Photographing her in the mountains was a much more difficult challenge as there are only 2-3 locations where tiger and habitat can be shown together. This is simply due to the sheer scale of the mountains above; all our photography was from vehicles so angles were very limited. Gradually though, as you will see in this book, we started getting good images of Noor

in the mountains. One superb location eluded us constantly though and we never managed to get her crossing it, she was always a few steps ahead of us. However we did manage to get one of her almost independent cubs walking through it, we wanted to include it in this book to show the diverse habitat that Noor and her family calls home.

Ranthambhore has the single largest expanse of dry-deciduous *Anogeissus pendula* forest left intact in India. It's a spectacular habitat to see tigers, perhaps one reason why Ranthambhore is considered by many to be the best place to see them in India. Again as photographers we have worked together to find different ways to show the habitat and one use throughout this book has been with monochrome photography. It's a challenge to get right, but when you do, the tones and atmosphere are hard to match anywhere else.

Here, in the still of a spring morning, we found Noor at peace with everything, sitting in the middle of a forest track just watching her domain. Jungle babblers babbled excitedly, peacocks gave their strangled mating calls and all around us the forest was alive with life. Right in the middle was its

Queen, doing nothing in particular… but always alert. We have spent many, many hours just sitting and waiting with Noor to get images like the one you see opposite. As you see here we always try to maintain a respectful distance, it's important for everyone to be relaxed, whether

they have stripes or otherwise! We have a superb team of drivers and guides for Ranthambhore; their skill and expertise allows us to concentrate on our photography and helping our clients make their dreams come true.

Caves play an important role in any tiger's life as they provide shelter and a cool place to hang out. Noor has a plethora of caves in her territory, we know anecdotally that she has given birth and nursed her very young cubs in several. This prominent cave near Kala Khet in Zone 2 is a favourite in any season but especially during the late spring into summer.

Caves give us a wonderful opportunity to really include some sexy mountain habitat. Above on the left you can see Noor having a much needed drink, then a stretch after a long snooze. On the right you can see a new generation using the cave; one of her most recent cubs who gave us 5 minutes of pure joy.

Winter in Ranthambhore is cold yet the light is magical. It can be a tough time to find Noor as she has lots of water choices inside the forest as the monsoon has only just finished, but when we do find her - wow!

Here the last rays of low winter sun penetrate the canopy to illuminate Noor as she relaxes in a waterhole; her eyes shine with a life that knows its purpose.

In contrast to the soft light and relatively pleasant temperatures of winter, summer is pure hell in the mountains. The heat is oppressive, approaching 50°C and Noor spends a lot of time sleeping during the day. Most hunts are at night, as are most movements, so any encounters we get in the first light of morning or the last rays of evening are to be savoured as they are rare periods of non-slumbering activity – this cat likes her sleep!

When we first started talking about this book, like so many other projects with a beer around a campfire, we knew that the photography would be tough. Noor lives in a very difficult territory to photograph, she has a lot of territory to roam within that is completely inaccessible to us. Even when we can see her, the terrain and the sheer scale of the geography often make photography impossible. So we have learnt to use our creative talents to make the most of the habitat, to embrace it and make the most of every single moment of her life that Noor shows us. So you will see in this book many images that show the habitat, and very few "postcard" shots of tigers.

The two shots here are prime examples of that. Opposite you can see Noor in a forest, as that is where we usually see her. Rather than take shots without the forest we wanted to show it, hence the interesting composition here that uses vegetation to hide parts of her body and make the final shot much more interesting. This is how we see her, hidden, watching, if she stood in the open then she would not be the successful hunter that she is.

Above, a different shot, eye contact with a ruthless killer. She uses her experience and intimate knowledge of the terrain to hide and wait when hunting; here she's down near a waterhole and flat behind a tree. Rather than rushing in like so many others do, we sit and think about the situation, opting for the best composition. Here it was to use the tree to create the ultimate *Eye of the Tiger* composition.

She watches and waits, muscles tensed and eyes fixed, each step forward taken painstakingly slowly. On her legs and other parts of her body she has tiny hairs to detect the ground that allow her to make a careful step without any sound and without having to take her eyes off the unsuspecting prey. It's a terrifying skill from a supreme hunter.

After the stalk comes the charge. Brutal. Aggressive. She reaches full speed in just a few strides, powering towards her fleeing prey, eyes still fixed and determined. It's just a matter of time before the inevitable…

Tigers have defined territories that they reinforce by constant patrolling and scent marking. Noor is no exception and spends a lot of time patrolling her large territory, usually this is a very peaceful experience and nothing prepared us for the amazing events that unfolded one summer morning.

The fight you see had been brewing for days as Noor's neighbour, T60 Ghost had brought her three cubs to a waterhole right on the edge of their territorial boundary. Tensions were high when out of nowhere both tigers rushed at each other, reared up and exchanged blows. The noise was terrifying and so was the ferocity of the fight. It was over in seconds but the memories will last in us forever.

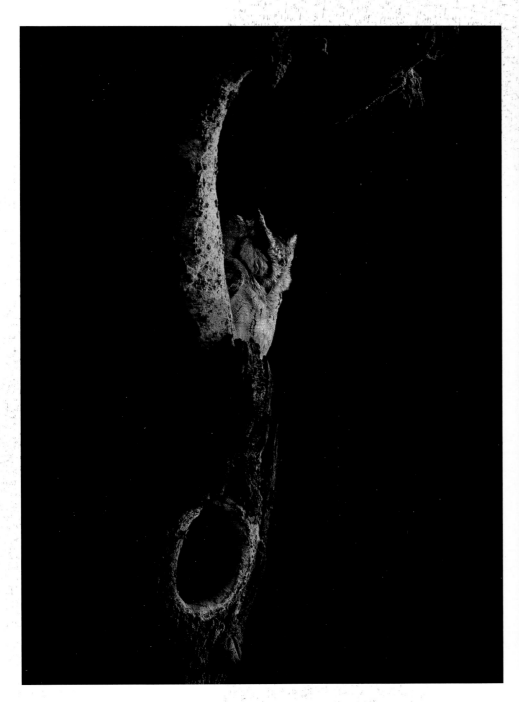

Noor shares her territory with a good population of leopards, as the rock-strewn habitat and proliferation of caves is perfect for their way of life. Perfect except for the fact that Noor absolutely hates them. We have watched her graduate from taking their kills to killing them at every opportunity… then eating them. Since every leopard sighting is a special one we always take the opportunity to photograph them; on this occasion the leopard had climbed the tree to escape the attentions of a sub-adult cub that had great fun chasing it up there! Like mother like daughter.

Ranthambhore is known for tigers but it has a great diversity of wildlife. Despite the tough, unforgiving habitat, the forests and dry river valleys are alive with tremendous birdlife, deer and the ever-present langur monkeys. Since most of our time is spent watching and waiting for Noor, we've managed to record some of the other species she lives alongside. Here you can see a Collared Scops Owl in its nest and a young Grey Langur Monkey backlit in the morning sun. Elusive but beautiful, and a vital part in the story of Noor's life.

Noor's dynasty

We think that Noor was born early in 2008 in the Tapkan area between zones 1 and 2 to a female called T13 and the male T12. Throughout this book you will see reference to these T numbers for tigers; they are unique numbers given to each tiger when they reach maturity. Some have more common names that are adopted by everyone, for example T39 is known better as Noor!

When Noor was over 2 years old her father was relocated to Sariska Tiger Reserve; soon his territory was taken over by another male T24, Ustad. This prompted Noor's mother to move to an area close to the current zone 10 to protect her next litter of cubs. After her passing, Noor soon took over her mother's old territory and continues to dominate it to this day.

Noor grew up with a brother, T38, who is now the dominant male of Kuno wildlife sanctuary in Madhya Pradesh. We have few easily identifiable images from this time, so on this page you can see some portraits of her as a young cub taken in 2009; note the trademark stare and stalking pose which you will come to recognise throughout this book.

Above, you can see Noor and her brother together caught in an affectionate moment, and one of her brother taken just before he moved out of the area; something that is common with young males to avoid conflict with their fathers.

Sultan

Noor's first litter was a single male cub called Sultan T72, born in the early spring of 2012. His father was the magnificent male Ustad (T24), of which you will hear more about later in this book. As a single cub Sultan was able to benefit from a fair share of any kills, thus he quickly grew into a big sub-adult tiger and started to hunt for himself from 18 months onwards. He was tolerated in Noor's territory, even when she had her second set of cubs, before eventually being driven out by his father Ustad. He was a great favourite to all of us due to his habit of approaching jeeps and his total disregard for their presence; to us he had an almost comical feel, looking like the complete package but acting like a teenager all the time.

Our story of Sultan has a happy ending. This camera trap image shows Sultan relaxing in a waterhole in Keladevi Sanctuary on the northern boundary of Ranthambhore National Park. He is the dominant male here and so we are proud to show one of the first pictures of his cubs with female T92.

Tracking tigers once they have left the tourism zones of Ranthambhore was always a very difficult task. These days, thanks to the amazing efforts of local organisation Tiger Watch, who empower local villagers to manage their camera traps, we know so much more about these tigers. These villagers are in the boundary zones that are so often in conflict with tigers; the more we know and the more local help we have, then the better chance we have of the tigers surviving.

We would like to express our thanks to Tiger Watch for allowing us to use these images here and you can find out more about their work later in this book.

Noor has had two males in her life, T57 (left) and T24 Ustad (right).
Both are very different tigers in their personality, with T57 being shy and
elusive whilst Ustad was at times terrifyingly used to vehicles. Both have
a great story to tell, a sad one in the case of Ustad, which you will hear
more of later in this book.

Noor's second litter (left) consisted of two males; Kaliya and Dholiya, born in the spring of 2014. This was the last litter fathered by Ustad. You will see them in an amazing portfolio next in this book but here on the left is an image to whet your appetite.

Noor's third litter died young in the den.

Noor's fourth litter consisted of three females and is seen here on the right, drinking in the winter of 2016. Fathered by the shy male T57 they are now fully independent, albeit still sub-adults but too young to get names or T-numbers. In the later portfolios of this book you will live their lives with them as they grow into adulthood; it's a wonderful and tender journey that we are so pleased to share with you.

First encounters

We'd never really concentrated much on Noor before; all our photographic endeavours had been geared towards Machali and then her daughter Sundari T17. After we had worked together on the successful tiger book *Tigers a Celebration of Life*, a few years elapsed before we could shoot together again as a team. In fact it was the tigress Sundari and her three small cubs that introduced us inadvertently to Noor. These cubs were rock stars and showing very well on zone 3, so we decided to start our cubs project on them as both of us had a lifelong desire to document the lives of a family from young cubs to independence. Unfortunately everyone else had the same plan and on the day we were due to begin, the Forest Department closed all access to zone 3 to allow Sundari to bring up her cubs in peace. It was the right choice of course, as the first thought must always be to the tigers, but it meant that we had to make other plans…

There had been some rumours that a tigress called Noor had been seen with teats in zone 2 and therefore must be nursing small cubs. It was neither a zone nor a tiger that either of us were too keen on but we had no choice, if we wanted cubs then Noor it had to be.

And so on the first day our adventures with Noor began, and our first joint trip into her zone made us both feel like we had stepped back in time. It was a complete contrast to the lush lake habitats we were used to with Machali and Sundari. It looked like a forgotten land, dominated by towering mountains. It was a rock-strewn landscape that instantly appealed to our photographic hearts. Little did we know at the time, it was the start of a love affair with these mountain zones that continues to this day.

Like any love affair it took a while to get started, with Noor being very elusive. In fairness there were a lot of vehicles in zone 2, since 3 was now closed, so we started to second guess her and wait in places away from the crowds. People thought we were mad, clueless, because we waited away from everyone else and away from the usual places. But Noor was clearly avoiding all the jeeps too and both of us are experienced enough with big cat behaviour to know that the obvious plans rarely succeed. Eventually she rewarded us for our patience; our first real encounter yielded us one quick walking image and the waterhole image opposite but even that was obscured by the bushes (a technique we would learn to use to our advantage). It was a success but we were already thinking that this would be a very tough trip indeed and that we had no chance of seeing the cubs; oh how little did we know…

We learnt a lot about Noor in the first few encounters with her, brief that they were. The first personality trait we observed was that she hated all things crocodile. Anytime she was close to the water, or if she saw the merest ripple, she would produce a fearsome snarl, lips curled back and a warning there for all to see. Anytime we have seen her coming to drink she looks uncomfortable, clearly sometime in her past she has had a bad encounter with one of our reptilian friends and she's never forgotten it. We also learnt that she's incredibly agile and fast, more so than any tiger we've ever seen. Bounding down this rock face left us all speechless and even to this day we both look up there and wonder how she did it

When we've sat down with a beer to talk about what makes Noor special to us, the same thought comes to both of us; it's the way she fixes us with her trademark Noor stare. Few other tigers stare directly at us, but Noor gives us stares that send shivers through our very core. It's this intensity about her that we love so much, as photographers it gives us portraits that are alive and which jump from the page. Later in this book you can see that our clients, who have shared so many experiences of Noor with us, think along similar lines as us with regards to her trademark stare. Two of these "stares" you can see here - on the left a contemptuous look as she sits in the water, on the right a much more menacing look as she stops her drinking to stare intently. Nothing triggered these looks, we are silent and still when we are with her, she just does it and we love her so much for it. It's rare for a tiger to connect like this, but that is the wonder of Noor, Queen of Ranthambhore.

After a few blank mornings our Noor quest was not going to plan so we decided to gamble and explore along a rocky valley that led to some remote waterholes. Noor was in the area and was certainly hiding somewhere. As we rounded the corner we saw her ahead in the rocks and something higher up caught our eyes. Was it a small tail that we saw running for shelter? We were convinced that we'd seen it, but was it just wishful thinking? Noor was sitting at the base of the rocks with a fresh kill next to her but she made no attempt to eat it. Instead she just stared up at the rocks above, pulling back her cheeks occasionally making an almost imperceptible sound. She never took her eyes off the rocks and when she did stare at us the message was clear… don't mess with me! After a while she covered the kill, using her paws to pull down vegetation with surprising dexterity. It was a very unusual thing for any tiger to do, after which she headed up the rocks and out of sight. Since we were alone we decided to leave immediately to keep her secret safe. Dicky reported it to the Forest Department and they closed all access to the road. Again not great for our photography but the most important thing was the safety of Noor and her cubs so they did the right thing.

A week passed and we saw Noor twice more. Sultan, Noor's first born male cub, was still in the area and gave us some fun but we really wanted to see Noor again. After yet another fruitless morning we re-entered the zone that afternoon expecting nothing; it was cloudy and the atmosphere was one of gloom. As we crossed the entrance to the rocky valley a jeep was parked there and quickly they beckoned us in. What followed was the most amazing hour of our lives and an encounter that not only started our relationship with Noor, but which will form the backbone of this book. Sit back with a drink and enjoy the most incredible tiger encounter you can imagine…

As we carefully and slowly approached we could see a tiny face staring at us from the safety of a cave. She had cubs! OMG!!!! Then we saw a second cub, having a merry time playing in a small pool of water. Noor was clearly stressed about them being separated so we immediately stopped a long distance away, which would prevent anyone else from going closer too. Mind made up she chased the errant cub, who made a valiant effort to get away for one last splash, before cornering it on the edge of another pool. We didn't know what would happen next. Slowly Noor bent down and when she turned round she had the cub gently picked up in her jaws… then she started walking towards us. It was simply incredible, adrenaline surged through our veins as Noor continued to do the unthinkable, it was the best waking dream of our lives. Onward she came and right by us she walked, there was a priceless look on the cub's face like a naughty schoolchild…

All was silent. We just stared at each other in disbelief; words could not express what we just saw. Tigers just don't do that in public, it was rare as rare could be and she had done it right in front of our jeep. By now a few jeeps had assembled so we made the decision to try to move everyone away from the cave to give Noor space. It seemed obvious that the only place she would come back to, if she came out again, was the pond as the cubs clearly were in the mood for play. Plus it was a humid afternoon. Luckily we had a good friend there, Balendu Singh, who helped us get the message out to everyone that silence was the key to Noor coming back out. The only hiccup was that one jeep got stuck on the rocks and was revving to get out, we pulled next to it and loaded the two Indian photographers into our jeep and told the driver to switch off. Suddenly the jeep was crowded but it was a decent thing to do, for them and for Noor.

Then we waited and waited. An hour passed and still no movement. Then a face appeared in the cave and out strode Noor, closely followed by the two tiny bundles behind. They disappeared in the grass but were clearly headed our way. When they appeared along the track it was immense, she gave her trademark "hate everyone" look at us whilst walking towards the water's edge. The two cubs looked on from behind and we thought that this would be it, just a quick drink and off. But Noor had other ideas. The waking dream continued unfolding in front of our eyes. She started to get into the water, and so began an encounter that was published worldwide for all to see… turn the page and you will be more in love with Noor than you could imagine.

There is no other phrase to describe any of this! We were shaking with excitement. It lasted over an hour. In the end Noor raised herself from the water and headed back to the grasses. She emerged on the other side and just stood there watching us, the cubs looking through her legs and even venturing out to her side. It was a wonderful goodbye and a perfect end to one of the most special wildlife encounters of our lives. She turned and led them to the cave and that was the end. The jeep was quiet as we were totally drained of emotion, it had been the most intense photographic hour of our lives; both of us just sat there in quiet contemplation. Then, as the Boss started the jeep to head home, we just turned and smiled at each other; it was a smile of two friends sharing an incredible experience together.

Tigers just do not give that kind of encounter. Yet Noor had laid everything that was most precious to her right in front of us. We worked well as a team that day, bouncing ideas off each other and shooting with different kit to give a different look and feel to the images. We've contributed equally to the pictures in this chapter, but of course you won't know whose is whose and that's the point. This encounter really taught us something about Noor; that she is a very special tigress and from that point we knew that she would be our muse, our favourite tiger to work with and the one we went the extra mile to see. Since then too, we've worked well as a team; no jealousy of the other one being in a great position when perhaps one is blocked, just admiration and happiness that we share it together. Our journey with Noor had begun and little did we know then what treasures were to come.

Ustad, from king to lifelong sadness

The story of the male Ustad, or T24, is one with a very sad ending. We both loved Ustad but Dicky was particularly close to him so here is the story in his words:

"Ustad or T24, as he is officially known, was born around 2006-07; one of the three male cubs of a tigress numbered T22. He grew up to be the most controversial tiger that Ranthambhore has ever had. When he was still looking for his territory after separating from his mother, a dominant male tiger numbered T12 (whose range included all of Noor's territory) was relocated to another tiger reserve in Rajasthan in order to repopulate it. So Ustad got an instant opportunity to occupy a large range that was left vacant by T12's removal and he grabbed it. Subsequently he sired Noor's first two litters, Sultan, and Kaliya and Dholiya; images of which you have seen in the previous portfolio of this book.

We all loved seeing Ustad as he was such an impressive tiger, so big and powerful, with a look that would wither and tell you your place in his world. I remember my first real encounter with him with Andy in the jeep. We managed to get ahead of the crowds that were following him, and in a stunning piece of driving from Himmat 'The Boss' Singh we reversed most of the way up the entrance road to zone 2 with Ustad walking a decent distance in front of us. We'd stop some way ahead and usually around a corner to wait for him to come. Slowly, yet purposefully, he'd appear round the corner and fix us with a gaze that told us in no uncertain terms to move! Andy, who is usually quiet and reserved when shooting tigers as he's so focussed, was ebullient, he could not believe the intensity that Ustad carried with him.

Ustad gave me many great experiences and I owe him for this image you see opposite, which won me the prestigious Sanctuary Asia Wildlife Photography Award in 2011. It was an incredible encounter; the Sloth Bear had two cubs on her back and refused to back down. The noise coming from Ustad was terrifying, he was really angry. In the end they both backed off, snarling and spitting all the way. Ustad was such a magnificent male tiger; I really wish that I had taken every chance to see him in the wild, as his life was about to change…

Just before he took over T12's range, he attacked, killed and partly ate a villager in early July 2010. At that time he was fitted with a radio-collar for research purposes and the researchers positively identified the man-eating tiger as T24. In 2012 he killed another young man and ate the carcass. Each of these killings was followed with violent protests by villagers demanding that the tiger be shot dead. In October 2012 he killed a forest guard, who was working to repair forest tracks with a group of people inside the tiger reserve. Two and a half years later he killed another forest guard at the edge of the reserve. All these four attacks were classic 'stalk and kill' actions where the man was killed after a fatal bite to the neck.

What followed after the fourth attack was an outcry that Ranthambhore had never seen before. The forest guards went on a strike and refused to work inside the reserve, unless Ustad was moved to a zoo, as they were worried about their personal safety. The local people living around Ranthambhore tiger reserve wanted the tiger taken out of Ranthambhore. A few days later, it was decided by the authorities to move Ustad to an enclosure in distant Udaipur, a fate worse than death for a wild tiger.

This decision to move the tiger to an enclosure created an unforeseen outcry in the Indian media. Activists and random people from different parts of India refuted the charge that Ustad had killed four people and demanded that he be left alone. Blatantly false stories were circulated about Ustad in mainstream and social media and his past history was forgotten. Some part of the mainstream media in India tried to portray that the 'tourism lobby' in Ranthambhore wanted to remove this tiger because they were scared that one of their tourists would be attacked. They claimed that this lobby provided the authorities with false evidence to remove the tiger. These stories ignored the fact that the decision to move Ustad to an enclosure was made by the highest authorities in the state of Rajasthan. There was no doubt that Ustad killed all these four people and ate two of them. The only reason he did not eat the other two was because a lot of people arrived at the locations to recover the bodies before he could start eating. There are hundreds of eyewitnesses, photographs and videos of all the four events. A legal case was filed in multiple courts in India to release Ustad back within Ranthambhore but this case was struck down by all the courts. This furore went on for a few months and then died down of its own accord.

I reached the sites of three of his four kills within an hour of Ustad killing the person, so I was able to witness the aftermath first hand. I strongly believe that a wild predator has to be strongly dealt with when they start killing humans as prey, as they are all over the world. All of us involved in this book strongly believe that the worst punishment that one can give to a wild predator like a tiger is to put them in captivity. It is far better to put them to sleep and this is the stand that we took. As a result of our stand, my family and I were abused on social media for months and received all sorts of threats. We calmly ignored them, as we knew we had the best interests of Ustad at heart.

To this day the once magnificent Ustad still languishes in his concrete prison, a shadow of his former self. One can only imagine his state of mind, to be stripped of everything that made him the tiger that he was. We both thought long and hard about including this section in this book, but we were determined that Ustad's story be told and that he was remembered as the amazing wild male tiger that you see here. If Noor was the Queen of Ranthambhore then he was certainly the King."

The sad demise of T24 Ustad caused a vacuum that was readily filled by another male tiger called T57. He is a very different tiger from Ustad; to be honest we were all uneasy around Ustad. We are certainly not relaxed around T57 as he has had his moments, but he's generally a very cool male tiger. The aggression that you see here was the only time we've ever seen it, and it wasn't directed at us either. But it showed that he was a true male tiger and since then we've watched T57 grow from a pretty scrawny male into the mighty beast that he is today; long may he rule the mountains.

Two years pass, a return

It was two years before we could shoot together again. Noor's two cubs, Kaliya and Dholiya had reached adulthood and departed the territory - no doubt with some "encouragement" from their mother involving much baring of teeth. There were rumours that Noor had a new set of cubs as she'd been seen with teats; this time somewhere in the hills of zone 1, but they were only rumours. As we'd later find out, this was her third litter and the one that she lost at a young age. So we came together again to work our magic and roll the dice with Noor, and like always she took us in a completely different direction than what we expected.

She was incredibly elusive during the first part of the trip, so we turned our attention to the neighbouring tiger T60 Ghost, and her cubs; it allowed us to keep our trigger fingers active but keep an eye on Noor's favourite hotspots. As always with Noor it looked bleak… then out of nowhere she blew our minds.

Early one morning we found her purposefully walking along the main track. She was clearly in a hunting mood. Knowing that every kill was vital to her; especially as we thought she might have cubs, we parked well ahead of her path, to give her room to see any opportunities. Noor is a very dynamic hunter. Whilst some may think her habitat is a tough one for hunting, she thrives there as she has learnt to adapt to the terrain and use the element of surprise. All tigers have different hunting methods; Noor seems to have mastered every single one. She can ambush in leopard style or run like a cheetah after her prey, either way once she has set her mind to it we have rarely seen her miss. But to be honest we had rarely photographed any of the hunts, as they always happened in bushes, behind a rock… you get the picture.

Perhaps today would be our lucky day…

We watched as she strode onto the rocky valley, froze, stared intently and at the same time we heard a few rocks falling behind us; her eyes widened, ears pricked up and she was away. Powering into a full speed run and bounding effortlessly across the boulder field she made ground with every stride on the fleeing Sambar deer. With a final leap she grabbed hold of the Sambar and used her weight to stop it. We estimated it had taken less than 20 seconds from start to finish, to us it seemed like slow motion; our hearts were pounding with excitement as the adrenaline surged through our veins.

Noor used her bodyweight to hang onto the Sambar and bring it down, before suffocating it. She'd perfected this hunting technique and it was incredible to see it first hand, right there in front of us. We've both seen many animals at the point of death, where the light fades from their eyes and the past semblance of life leaves their body. Today was no exception, Noor kept her deadly grip until she was sure that all life had passed.

The heat was now increasing by the minute so she grabbed the heavy deadweight of the Sambar (around 160 kg) and hauled it straight up the slope. It was an amazing feat of strength; she was so incredibly strong. She then pulled it into the same cave where she had been two years previously with the cubs, and immediately started to feed. Our time ended and we had to leave her to it. Noor had delivered for us and once again we were the only ones to see it. Our incredible relationship with Noor was going from strength to strength, could it get any better?

In the afternoon we were first on scene as we expected her to still be feeding but the cave was empty with no sign of a feeding or snoozing tiger. So we decided to check the local waterhole…

The waterhole was a beautiful one and there sitting in it was an equally beautiful tiger. But it wasn't Noor. It was a new male on the scene; T57. A very different tiger from Ustad, he had taken over the territory and everything that came with it, including

an aggressive, intense, and thoroughly awesome tigress called Noor! He seemed relaxed and we wondered if he'd stolen her kill and pushed her away. Or perhaps, as we'd hoped, she'd returned to the cubs and was currently bringing them to the kill.

Knowing that deer alarm calls from the forest would warn us of her impending approach, we opted to stay with T57 and he obliged by moving slightly closer to us to be under the shade of the tree. Then we realised that actually he wasn't alone…

Noor had been there all along, hidden where we could not see, sleeping in the shade. She came and sat close to him at the waterhole. Clearly she had no cubs as it had been days since she had been back to zone 1 (as we were to find out later they had perished in the den). Male and female tigers generally only come together for one thing, and although we never caught them in the act, it was obvious that she was receptive to his approaches. When she got out to leave the waterhole he followed her a few minutes later, demonstrating the flehmen gesture to pull her scent across special glands and no doubt check that she was in season. Making an unwelcome approach to Noor would be a painful experience, we were sure of that. We didn't see either of them again the whole trip, they vanished into the Tapkan area where we could not follow. Tapkan, you may remember, was the exact area where Noor was born.

It was only several months later, after the monsoon, that we found out why they had gone there…

Leopards

No one really knows what happened to Noor's third litter, it's a well-known fact that tiger cubs are at their most vulnerable during the first few months of life. Leopards are great opportunists and will kill any other predator's young if they get the chance. It's why so many other big cats hate leopards and go out of their way to chase them off if found. The cubs were never found so nothing is known about their fate, but it is an area with a high leopard population so perhaps that is one explanation.

Ranthambhore is not well known for its leopards, but in the mountain zones that Noor calls home they were relatively common. We used to see them a fair amount, at least once per week and we went through a period where it was once per day. Interestingly this was during the time when Noor had 6 month old cubs, big enough to defend themselves against any leopard attack. Several times we witnessed her stealing fresh kills that had been made by leopards.

Since that time we have seen a marked decrease in leopards in Noor's territory and sightings are now much more rare and fleeting. Leopards have become less bold, and seem to be sticking to the mountain areas where they feel safe. Safe? Yes safe. From Noor. We have heard from several guides we trust that Noor has been seen carrying dead leopards and more than that, actively eating their carcass with her cubs. This is pretty unheard of, but Noor makes a point of killing them and eating them. Knowing Noor as we do, this can only be a deliberate act; sure she is an opportunist but it seems as if she is taking particular interest in the leopard population in her core area. The evidence for this is only hearsay from people we trust within the park - there is no firm evidence, but one thing is for sure, there are far fewer leopards seen now in Noor's core territory than ever before.

Winter in Ranthambhore

Winter in Ranthambhore is a special time for us as the light is exquisite. It's a photographer's playground. Whilst the mornings are absolutely freezing, even to those of us from European climes, once the light bathes everything in a warm orange glow all is good in the world. Everything looks at its best in the winter; tigers of course shine in the orange light but so do the deer species who have their thick coats. The low light allows us to create more atmospheric images; something which is really important to us in this project, as we want to show Ranthambhore in all its glory.

The monsoon passed and for much of October Noor was absent and very hard to find. Then she was seen with new and obviously fresh teats, and a week later with small cubs at a distance. Clearly T57 had done his job and fathered his first litter with Noor. We were ecstatic, like proud grandparents, and we knew that with a lot of hard work we had a chance over the coming weeks to see them. It had been a good monsoon so there was water everywhere in the park. Great for tigers, but not so great for us as she had a lot of choice where to go. But it was Noor, and we knew that as our muse she would deliver for us, we just had no idea how much!

The first few days we found her constantly patrolling her territory, stopping to scent mark on prominent trees and just covering those easy miles that tigers do. Here you can see a couple of images of Noor on patrol in the beautiful winter light. She had a set routine, we'd get on her for a while then she would vanish, but always in roughly the same place. It was obvious to us that she had the cubs stashed somewhere there. It was just a matter of time and patience, we kept trying, kept searching and one morning it all came right again…

All the patrolling was actually great for our photography, as she looked wonderful in the winter light. Since we are Noor specialists (some call us obsessives) we know her routes and can therefore second guess where she will walk. This means we can be there waiting and let her come by, that way we don't disturb her patrolling but we get to show the world how beautiful she is.

Throughout this book we've tried not to show average tiger pictures, shot in the middle of the frame with bad composition. We feel that as Noor lovers it's our job to show her in the best light. Sometimes, as you see here, we use natural frames like grass or trees to show the habitat that she lives in. It's a technique that works well… provided you can find her in the first place!

The morning had been a good one. We'd started off with zone 3 rock star female Arrowhead plodding along a track in the early light, had a quick encounter with T60 Ghost and had found ourselves in Noor central just as the park was emptying of the normal tourists. We knew from experience that she rarely moves early and that certainly she would not bring the cubs out until it had warmed up, so there was method in our madness. Sure enough we were rewarded; checking a waterhole we quickly saw a cub scampering off and there was Noor watching us from the grass. She strode out, but away from us, and headed towards a rock face with the cub in tow.

She sat against the rock face which gave us the chance to shoot some interesting wide-angle habitat shots. As we've said before, it's rare in Noor land to do this as the habitat is not the kindest to shooting wide angle so we feasted at the chance. The cubs kept us smiling with their antics; swinging off a hanging vine and the video we shot is priceless but that will be for another time.

Then, as always, she decided enough was enough and disappeared into the hills behind. She was gone for another two days, not even an alarm call, but we knew to keep up the pressure on ourselves. Then, late one morning, it was BOOM… all over again…

A winter morning we will never forget

Noor had clearly been on territorial patrol and needed a long drink; it soon became a family fun time, as you will see over these coming pages.

Another magic encounter that Noor shared with us, and another where it was just her and us. It was becoming a habit, and we loved it, who knew what she would have in store next!

The stunning light of winter also allows us to express ourselves photographically with the other wildlife that lives alongside Noor and her family. The low light in the forests allows us to really push the boundaries and create atmospheric images of Langur Monkeys, Sambar Deer and even Mugger Crocodiles. Tigers aren't the only beautiful species in Ranthambhore.

Spring

Spring in Ranthambhore is a wonderful time, as it's the bridge between the lovely pastel colours and comfortable temperatures of winter and the searing hot misery of summer. All around the park flowers begin to bloom and trees begin to change colour. It's a time for young animals throughout the park too, which is of course a good thing for the resident predators.

After the winter's escapades with the cubs we had high hopes for the coming of spring, as the cubs would be older and much more mobile. As you will see, it didn't disappoint. As usual though it took us a while to get into the pace of what Noor was doing. Unlike the winter when she was elusive, we found Noor almost every single day, usually patrolling her territory alone first thing in the morning. The two images opposite are some of our favourites from these early morning encounters, they both have the trademark "death" stare from her and they are most definitely Noor!

Our morning encounters though, whilst wonderful, could not compare with what Noor shared with us during the late mornings and early afternoons of each day. It was simply magical and mostly we shared it solely with her; again she showed us what was most precious to her in the world.

So sit back and feast your eyes on an amazing period in her life, and to be honest, ours too.

She liked to move them to a new area regularly, every couple of days at least, and for us it generally meant the start of an epic hour or two. It was interesting to see her choice of location for the cubs when they were young, she stuck to the forests of zone 1 and the mountain valleys that led into zone 2, but rarely took the cubs into zone 2 itself. Perhaps it was the forest cover and better shelter from the midday heat; one thing was sure though, we'd always find her there or thereabouts. The walks would always start the same way, she would gather the cubs together and let them have some communal play before suddenly standing up, stretching and moving off with them nuzzling close to her.

The walks along the forest tracks were amongst our most memorable encounters as it was generally her and us, jeeps and tigers, working in perfect harmony. As she walked we always tried to get several hundred metres ahead of her, to give her space to breathe and the cubs to be relaxed. When she got close to the vehicles she'd tell us to move with the "death stare" for which she is known, the message was clear and always received!

During these road encounters we photographed very little play and mischief between the cubs. We are both experienced big cat photographers and used to watching the antics of lion and cheetah cubs of a similar age, but tigers are much more reserved. Maybe they just weren't relaxed enough in front of us, we will never know. As the weeks went by we noticed a definite personality change in the cubs, with one female always staying close to Noor as you can see here.

Eventually the cubs would start to spread out too much for her liking and she'd look for somewhere to stop for a while close to the road. This was usually the cue for some lovely interaction between the family and was a time that we always looked forward to seeing.

Often if she stopped on the road the boldest cub would come and approach our vehicles. We never moved away as starting the engine would have scared her; under the watchful gaze of Noor we just sat quietly. We'd get sized up, everything would be inspected and we definitely felt what it was like to be on the "other side".

After the intimate family moments the cubs would usually play and one of their favourite pastimes was tree climbing. They could not resist it and sometimes were many metres off the ground. It was so great to watch them do this, eventually though Noor always called them down and that would be the end of the encounter, she'd disappear into the forest to sleep and that was that!

These two pages show the developing contrast in their personalities. One was definitely very shy and kept close to Noor, you can see that above and in previous images in this book. The other two were becoming very bold, often striking out by themselves and showing some feisty behaviour like this mini snarl. Their boldness increased and during the walks they would often be well ahead of Noor, much to her obvious annoyance. More than once she greeted them with a fearsome snarl as if to tell them to toe the line. The increasing independence of the slightly larger of the two paid dividends one afternoon with its first kill. It was a chance encounter, the cub was walking ahead of Noor when it disturbed a deer fawn in the grass. Instinct took over immediately, and the cub chased and caught it, bringing it down in the forest. It's nature's classroom; learning how to survive in Ranthambhore is a skill that they would all have to master and we were privileged to witness the first steps.

These tender encounters were amazing to watch, we were used to seeing Noor as a fierce, uncompromising tiger, though here she was a tender mother, always watching and always loving to the cubs. Occasionally she'd fix us with a stare that showed us our place and sent us retreating behind our cameras. But mostly she'd ignore us and concentrate on the cubs, patiently cleaning them and tolerating their constant desire to play.

These are some of the final images we took in spring and marked a change in the family behaviour. The young were becoming increasingly independent and often walked apart, except for the one that stayed close to Noor. As the temperature rose Noor became a less frequent visitor to zone 1 and one day moved her cubs to zone 2; we managed to intercept her as she strode through the dark forests at the end of the day, setting up the cubs at the waterholes nearby. She never returned to zone 1 that season, preferring instead to be in zone 2 even though it was incredibly hot and unforgiving. Clearly she knew best, as she was the master of her home.

Spring was a great time for us with tigers but it's also a boom time for photographing the other species in the park. All the deer species have young, like the Chital that you see here; which makes photographing them so much more engaging. Cold blooded reptiles like this Monitor Lizard are seen in earlier light too, and were also more likely to sit still… for once.

Summer

Summer is oppressive and unrelenting in Noor's territory. The sun is so strong that it penetrates everything and shade is at a premium for predator and prey alike. The mountain valleys trap the heat and it's often 48-50 °C, tough for tiger and photographer alike. Tempers fray and the battle for territory intensifies as the acquisition of water is suddenly top priority.

Summer is not only tough for tigers but for photographers too. The light is harsh and unrelenting, making images look washed out. We wanted to somehow express this in our work but traditional landscapes in colour just didn't look right. We wanted to show this tough domain that Noor calls home in a way that has not been done before. So we both shot with specially modified cameras to capture infrared (IR) images. The best thing about infrared pictures is that you see a perspective that you have never seen before as humans cannot see infrared light at all. We found that trees glow white with the heat; everything looks washed out with intense light. Exactly what we wanted to achieve.

So we are starting this chapter with a mini portfolio of our summer IR work, you can see here two contrasting shots of Noor chilling out by the relative cool of a waterhole.

Noor sits in one of her favourite waterholes; a super-wide lens was used to get the dominant bluffs in too.

With IR cameras leaves turn bright white, giving the trees an etherial like quality.

A rock river and the beautiful waterhole of zone 1 look inviting in the heat of the midday sun.

Noor relaxing in the cooling waters. All tigers generally back in towards the water and prefer to sit facing the outside world. In Noor's case any entry to water was preceded by intense snarling as her total hatred of all things crocodile is never absent.

In the days when access was still allowed this was one of our favourite waterholes, now the Forest Department have given it back to Noor as a place she can escape to for peace and quiet.

Clearly suffering from the heat, Noor takes a shortcut though the forest.

Summer is a wonderful time to see the birdlife of Ranthambhore as water sources become limited which in turn concentrates the species within a small area. The usually elusive bird life of Noor's mountain territory becomes much easier to see and we love spending time at waterholes challenging each other to get increasingly more difficult shots.

Above you see a black tailed drongo drinking and opposite a green bee-eater and a male paradise flycatcher doing exactly the same. Of course with all this bird-life being close to water it's a great time to see the beautiful Shikra too...

As has been said already the summer is all about water, here you can see Noor making the most of the waterholes in her territory. The cubs particularly found it hard to cope, as it was their first summer.

Cubs being cubs, the cool of the evening brings about playtime and they delight us all with their antics, play fighting and arguing over possession of a stick that just happened to fall their way. It's so nice to see young tigers at play; totally relaxed and almost relieved at the relative cool of the evenings. It's a welcome relief for us too from the oppressive heat.

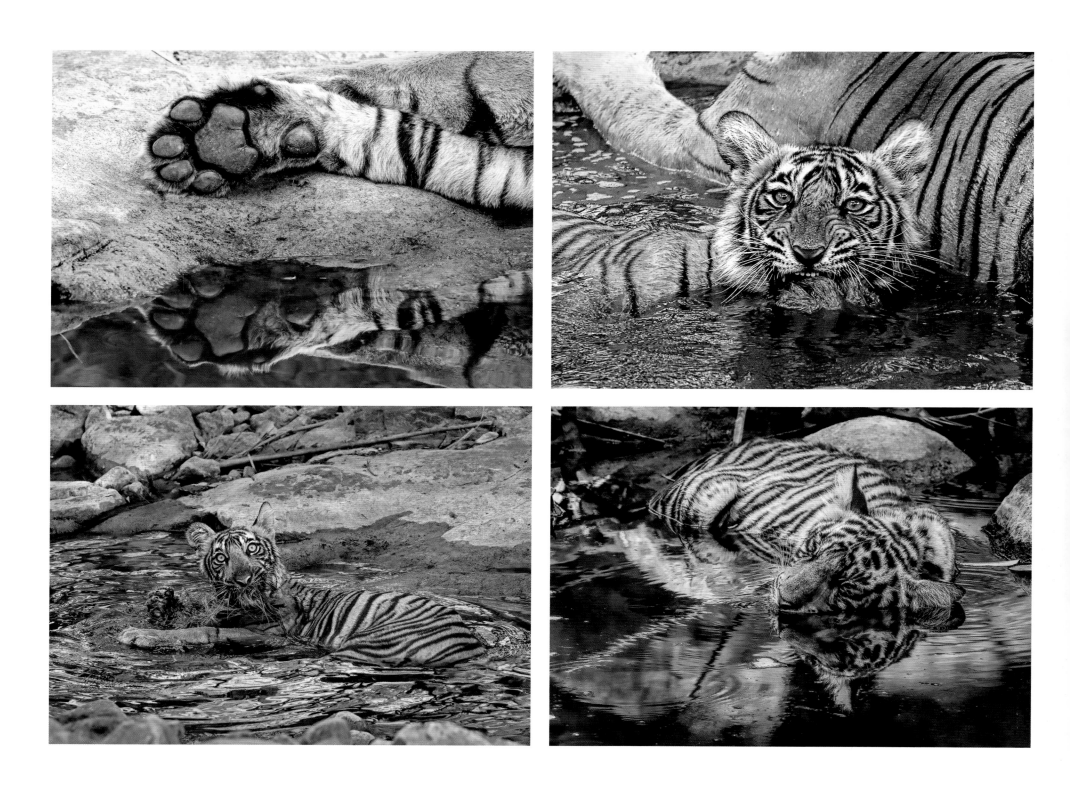

On really hot days, all activity is confined to the early morning or late at night. Here we found the whole family sleeping the day after they had finished a kill. Soon it would be time for Noor to hunt again, but until then there was only one thing to do… like we said, this tiger loves to sleep!

Two images to show the tenderness that Noor shows her cubs; particularly the female with whom she appeared to have a very strong bond, and who rarely left her side. It was such a beautiful moment to witness this affection, so much peace in the forest. Of course this peace and harmony would all be short lived, as the cubs got older and approached independence, tempers would flare and the relationship between Noor and her cubs would degrade completely. But for now it was all peace and harmony and we loved being there to see it.

Independence

Fast forward another 9 months and we found a complete change in Noor and her cubs. With one exception they were now a very disjointed family, with two of the cubs living apart from Noor for most of the time. The third cub, who if you remember from the spring images was always close to her, stuck much closer and was "tolerated". It had to be on Noor's terms though, any close approach might trigger a brutal one-sided fight. Noor always seemed to have a permanent snarl at this time; she was in a much worse mood than normal.

Aggression aside, which is entirely natural behaviour, she was still a great mother. Several times she killed and shared it with the cubs but no longer was there any communal dining; once Noor had finished and had moved off, the cubs fought it out. These are the shots we were waiting for to end this story of Noor and her 4th litter of cubs, just as we had done with Machali so many years earlier. Unfortunately despite us being there at the right time, Noor proved elusive and we saw no fights that we could even get near photographing. This is very Noor; if she wants to share

her life she does, if she doesn't then she's a ghost. We saw plenty of the cubs though, generally walking and establishing territory, or at least being "allowed" to establish territory. Several times we got some great activity in beautiful light; there was much familiarity with the way that both the more independent cubs went about their business. They were mini Noors and it was such a privilege to watch them finding their way in the world.

It's now really time to stop calling them cubs. They aren't, they are now officially sub-adults and at 24 months of age all will get their T-numbers from the Forest Department that will be used to accompany them through their lives. Day by day we watched as they explored and started to establish their own areas, you cannot think of them as territories yet as once they have

established full independence Noor might have other ideas. We'd only know after the monsoon who she allowed to stay and who she didn't, it was her choice.

These two images show how we wanted to show the sub-adults as they explored. Throughout this book we have enough

close-in images, which are a necessity due to the habitat in which Noor lives and the lack of roads. With two of the sub-adults free roaming we were given chances that we rarely had before, and could record them in lovely habitat style shots. In both cases we used the surrounding trees to create natural frames that perfectly framed these beautiful young tigers.

This was the last picture that we took on our Noor project as the cubs became difficult to see and Noor had all but vanished. Tigers often do this after the mating cycle is complete, it's a time of rest and to be alone before the next mating cycle begins.

It's a fitting end as it shows one of the cubs, the most independent and capable one, jumping an old dam on the entrance to the famous rocky valley. It's such a good feeling to see the little cubs that we saw when they were so young, grow into magnificent mature tigers. Yet again Noor has raised a litter successfully to adulthood, helping to ensure the survival of this incredible cat.

Our team is now preparing for the next challenge, to complete a similar project to this one except on Krishna and her rock star cubs. We've got a lot of material already; the icing on the cake will be if the ever willing Arrowhead gives birth to her first set of cubs. Time will tell. Of course we will never ignore Noor, she is too special to us for that, and a couple of times per week we will drop in and see what she is up to, as she is more to us than just another tiger. Who knows, she may have another litter, she's certainly young enough. She's the reason we became such lifelong friends and the reason that we learnt to work together so successfully, as few professional photographer collaborations ever work out.

But this book is not over yet, oh no, we have important things to say. First a look at tiger conservation and organisations that are playing a major role in it. Then it's a look at our photography skills with a mini technique workshop and finally it's the turn of our wonderful clients to show some of their favourite images of Noor.

We sincerely hope that you have enjoyed this book and following through her life with us. We've had the time of our lives working with Noor, shared incredible encounters, and have memories that will stay with us forever.

Noor, Queen of Ranthambhore.

Conservation

There are thirteen countries in the world where tigers are found in the wild and in each one of these countries, tigers are fighting a losing battle for their survival. The two biggest conservation threats that wild tigers face are habitat loss and poaching. Tigers are territorial cats that need forest cover, water and high density of prey animals to survive. Unfortunately, due to increasing human population and the resulting consumption, forest cover is decreasing at an alarming rate in the entire range where tigers exist. Barely one per cent of the historic range of tigers now has the kind of forest cover and prey base that can sustain breeding populations of tigers. Habitat loss is definitely the biggest threat that tigers face the world over. Poaching of tigers for their body parts is the second biggest threat to wild tigers. There is a huge demand for tigers' parts around the world and poachers will keep the supply going as long as the demand is there. Besides falling to poachers, a lot of tigers in the wild are killed by farmers and pastoralists as revenge for killing their cattle. While habitat loss usually happens over a longer period of time, poaching can, and has, wiped out tigers in small and large localised areas in a very short period of time.

Out of all the countries where tigers are found in the wild India has over half the world's tigers and the battle for tiger's survival will be decided in India. The two biggest problems that wild tigers face in India are the same - habitat loss and killing. India has a huge growing population in a relatively small land mass and there is a lot of human pressure on tiger habitats in India. In the last few decades, India enacted some strong wildlife protection laws keeping tigers as the main focus. The idea was that if we work on saving the tigers then we have to work on saving the entire tiger habitat. India started a very serious "save the tigers" campaign over four decades ago. Critics are quick to point out that the results of this campaign have not been great though we believe that the fact that tiger numbers are now stable and slowly rising is itself a great achievement, especially if we keep in mind that our human population has more than doubled since the start of the "save the tigers" campaign.

Like we said before, tigers are fighting a losing battle for their survival but there are a few bright spots in their struggle for survival and Ranthambhore is one such bright spot. Until a decade ago the forests of Ranthambhore could not sustain a population of more than 40-45 tigers. However, a well planned and sustained effort to increase the tiger habitat in the last decade or so, has led to a situation where Ranthambhore now has between 65 and 70 tigers. During the same time frame, scientific monitoring of tigers and anti-poaching intelligence gathering has drastically reduced the threat of poaching in and around Ranthambhore. At the same time, more tourism friendly rules created a strong pressure group of local people who benefit from tiger tourism. All these three factors worked in a combination that pushed the population of wild tigers in Ranthambhore to the highest ever. The battle goes on but the situation is now not as hopeless as it seemed just 15 years ago. The credit for this goes majorly to a dedicated team of forest officials working for Ranthambhore and local Non-governmental organisations and individual tiger activists.

The attitude of the local community living around tiger habitats plays a huge role in the well being of tiger populations. If locals do not want tigers in their backyard then there will be no tigers. In all the countries that have wild tigers, tigers are found in areas with the highest levels of poverty. However, tigers still exist in such areas because the locals here have a really small ecological footprint. Such people may not be as conscious about saving the tigers as many of us but they do have a far smaller ecological impact on the local environment than we do. Fortunately for the tigers, most people in India have a really high tolerance for wild animals in their backyard and this is one big silver lining for tigers in India.

Tiger Watch is an NGO with the core objective of protection of wildlife in and around Ranthambhore Tiger Reserve. It empowers local communities that are outside the protected area of the park with innovative programmes to track wildlife and monitor any poaching activities, taking positive action with the help of the Forest Department when needed. Research showed that people from a particular semi-nomadic community called Mogya are responsible for most of the poaching. Realising the need to mainstream the Mogya community to help end the poaching, Tiger Watch initiated the Mogya rehabilitation programme to provide them with health, education and livelihood, to show an alternative to revenue than from tiger poaching. With your support, Tiger Watch is looking to expand its work to fill the gaps and enhance the protection of wildlife of Ranthambhore.
Website: www.tigerwatch.net
Facebook: @tigerwatch

Using the tiger as a metaphor for all of nature, Wildlife Conservation Trust (WCT) has been envisioned to preserve and protect India's rich natural heritage. Currently, WCT works in and around 160 Protected Areas across 23 states in the country covering most of India's 50 tiger reserves besides other protected areas and impacting a population base of approximately 3.5 million people. WCT works towards the mitigation of anthropogenic pressures with a firm belief in landscape-level conservation of both wildlife and their habitats, sustainably factoring in the needs of people dependent on these forests.
Website: www.wildlifeconservationtrust.org
Twitter: WCT_India
Instagram: wctindia

WWF India has been working in and around Ranthambhore Tiger Reserve since the 90's and consolidated its conservation efforts into the Western India Tiger Landscape Programme in 2012. The landscape conservation approach looks beyond the boundaries of the Protected Areas, into the corridors and human dominated landscapes. WWF India has been working with the Rajasthan Forest Department and key stakeholders for monitoring tigers, co-predators and prey, and studying tiger dispersal patterns in four potential corridors connecting Ranthambhore with Keladevi, Kuno, Keladevi-Kuno, and Ramgarh-Mukundra. All these efforts have helped improve protection measures in the forest, and facilitate dispersal of tigers within the landscape. WWF India is committed to strengthening partnerships with the government and other implementing agencies.

TOFTigers
Sustaining the wild

TOFTigers is a pioneering collective action campaign and leader in advocating, planning and certifying sustainable tourism in South Asia as a wildlife conservation tool, with a 14 year track record and global membership of close to 300 travel companies. Our mission is to make nature tourism a force for good – protecting biodiversity, restoring habitats, supporting rural livelihoods and raising awareness of the vital role played by ecosystems from clean air, water security, flood prevention to food, medicines and ensuring our own mental, physical and spiritual wellbeing.
Website: www.toftigers.org
Twitter: TofTigersIndia
Facebook: www.facebook.com/toft.india

WILDCATS CONSERVATION ALLIANCE

WildCats Conservation Alliance (which in 2017 united 21st Century Tiger with Amur Leopard and Tiger Alliance) is a programme of the Zoological Society of London in partnership with Dreamworld Wildlife Foundation. They build on nearly 20 years' experience providing a safe, transparent method for money to be donated to conservation projects for wild tigers and Amur leopards by giving grants to projects that are carefully selected with the assistance of independent, expert reviewers. The projects are expected to follow best practice, have measurable objectives and scientific rigour.
Website: www.conservewildcats.org
Facebook: @conservewildcats
Twitter: @conservewildcat.

Panthera is devoted exclusively to preserving wild cats and their critical role in the world's ecosystems. Panthera's team of leading biologists, law enforcement experts and wild cat advocates develop innovative strategies based on the best available science to protect cheetahs, jaguars, leopards, lions, pumas, snow leopards and tigers and their vast landscapes. In 36 countries around the world, Panthera works with a wide variety of stakeholders to reduce or eliminate the most pressing threats to wild cats, securing their future—and ours.
Website: www.panthera.org
Instagram: @pantheracats
Facebook: @pantheracats
Twitter: @pantheracats

Save Wild Tigers (SWT) mission is to provide urgent and ongoing targeted support for tiger conservation in a bid to eradicate the increasing threat of extinction that wild tigers face. SWT uniquely uses its marketing and creative skill set to develop high profile global campaigns to help raise awareness around the critical issues and raise significant funds to help support tiger conservation programmes with our partners in India (Satpuda Landscape Tiger Programme), conservation programmes including anti-poaching initiatives in Malaysia via WCS and global cutting edge investigations by the EIA into the illegal trade in Tiger skins and parts.
Website: www.savewildtigers.org
Facebook: Save-Wild-Tigers-507934189245538
Instagram: @savewildtigers

Photography

Welcome to the Photo Zone! Hopefully you have all enjoyed the images in this book, well now we would like to give you an insight into how we took them. Here's some handy tips that you can apply to your photography wherever you are in the world, but first let's have a look at the kit that we have used in this book…

Everything you have seen in this book has been shot by us physically at the time, the only camera trap pictures are those from our friends at Tiger Watch. Whilst they have their place in photography, we both passionately believe that part of the joy of photography is actually being present at the time the action (or sleeping!) is happening.

As tiger photographers we have learnt to be flexible, sometimes tigers are close sometimes they are far. Therefore we need to have kit that can cover a wide range of possibilities without the need to change it, as speed is often the essence. So in general we both try to shoot most of our work with medium focal length zooms lenses, but hey, let's see what we say in our own words…

Andy - *"As a Canon Ambassador I use a combination of the 1-DX Mark II and 5D Mark IV bodies, with lenses including 24-70mm, 100-400mm, 200-400mm and 500mm. I also love using the mirrorless EOS M5 as it's small, light and great for shots from awkward angles due to its flip out screen".*

Dicky - *"I have always used Nikon kit and these days my main camera is the D5. In terms of lenses I try to shoot wherever possible with the Nikon 200-400mm as I love it. I always carry two Panasonic GH5 bodies as well to film movies, as I find they produce excellent 4K quality".*

As you know by now we both use infrared modified cameras too, but more on this over the coming pages. So now let's look at some of the techniques that we use to get our shots…

GETTING KILLER PORTRAITS

Focal length 400mm, ISO 800, f11 @ 1/250th

GETTING GREAT FAMILY PORTRAITS

Focal length 500mm, ISO 800, f8 @ 1/500th

We mentioned earlier in this book about Noor's killer look, it's enabled us to get relatively clean and good portraits of her as she looks right at us. When taking portraits of anything the trick is to keep everything simple, as the main subject, in this instance the tiger, must be the highlight. This means that a portrait is very unforgiving and there is nowhere to hide any mistakes, everything must be done perfectly.

First you need a decent depth of field to get sharpness from nose to ears, balanced with the need of course to keep the background relatively diffuse. One trick to help this is to shoot parallel with the subject, neither up nor down; another is to always use the biggest lens you can to flatten the facial features (that's just physics) and to keep that background at bay. This portrait was shot at the 400mm range with an aperture of f11, the depth-of-field preview button was used (check your camera manual) to ensure that f11 didn't include too much background.

Next you need to have the eyes wide open, not half closed or with shadows. This means shooting either in low light or in diffused light such as cloudy days or under a tree canopy. This is perhaps the toughest thing to do with tigers, and one reason why portraits of them are so tough.

Finally the composition; to be honest we always do this after in Photoshop as it's too emotional and too subjective at the time. Just choose the composition that looks right to you, don't adhere to any rules as they are made by someone else and it's your photography and vision that counts. With this image we left space to the right, which is a commercial composition for this book to allow a bleed across the page - as it turned out it didn't make the main book so proudly sits here!

We would say that the number one favourite encounter of every photographer and visitor to tiger land is when you get a mother with cubs. It has everything for the photographer, interaction, drama and the chance to take something that will truly impress your friends and family. We have documented Noor's relationship with her cubs throughout this book and you will see some lovely images (we hope!). Here's one that again didn't quite make it into the main book, but which we think worthy of inclusion here as it's got some important lessons to highlight. The first is about connection, clearly none of the cubs are looking at the camera but Noor is, this maintains the connection between the viewer and the image. Family portraits need to have some connection, either between the subjects themselves or the subjects and the viewer. Next it's the focus point; in situations like these it always needs to be on the closest point, which is the lead cub's face. To put it on Noor may render the cub out of focus unless a decent aperture is used, so it was safer in this case to stick to the closest point.

Finally this was a really difficult image to process. The sun was high and the canopy was thick as it was late spring, so the light was very, very flat. Portraits need to stand out and jump from the page to be effective, they need to grab you, and flat light certainly doesn't help with this. So images like this need post processing, they need to be lifted and made to stand out by giving them additional contrast. For this image we used an app called Topaz Clarity that gave a HDR/painting feel to the image and made the flat light less of an issue. It's a distraction technique really, the flat light is always there, we are just hiding a little. Good post processing is essential if you really want your images to stand out.

GETTING EFFECTIVE WALKING SHOTS

Focal length 400mm, ISO 800, f5.6 @ 1/500 for both

Both Ustad (left) and Noor (above) are patrolling their territories, which gives us a great chance to get walking shots. It's always really, really difficult trying to get walking pictures in Ranthambhore, as so many photographers just react to shooting what is in front of them, instead of planning for the best shot and thinking a few minutes ahead.

We always back off way ahead of the tiger's route, so we can get it at a distance with a flatter angle or coming over a small hill, either way it's a much better shot than crowding it. Alas, too many people who should know better, park next to the tiger and shoot down on it walking at an impossible angle, sometimes causing it unforgivably to leave the track. It's our hope that maybe our way of working, which shows tremendous respect to the tiger, can be adopted by a few more people than the handful of friends that use this method with us.

Technically speaking now, only shoot when it's perfect and pick the shot with the foot striding forward like you see here, as that is positive composition. Keep the aperture to f4/f5.6 which keeps enough detail on the tiger but blurs the background. Finally get connection. i.e. looking at you, and keep your distance as the image is much better!

CREATE SOMETHING SPECIAL, MAKE EACH CLICK COUNT

Focal length 500mm, ISO 400, f11 @ 1/500th

These two images show why it's good to ignore other people's rules and follow your own path. This image was shot when there was no light and no other shot. Rather than giving up we used a shutter speed of 1/15th second and panned the motion to create this cool effect; experimenting is cool!

There are hundreds of thousands of tiger images shot every month in Ranthambhore and other tiger reserves in India. It's fair to say that 99% of those taken are deleted, as we have watched an increasing number of photographers use the motor drive to get images, rattling away at full speed. Unfortunately if you adopt this method and you get the first image wrong then the next hundred will all be wrong too. Too many photographers want to look and sound good, but in reality this is meaningless; it's the images you produce that count, not what brand of camouflage clothing you are wearing. The best strategy is always to pick the images that you want and only hit the motor drive when you see something special. This means that you take your time with the composition and exposure, you become very selective. There seems to be a perception that you have to come away with loads of images to make it a successful trip, when actually it's better to have 10 awesome images that people like, than 100 awful ones that cause no reaction at all. So be selective and pick what you need.

Equally important to being selective is to try take images that are different from everyone else. Think outside of the box. Dare to be creative. Take this image for example. We both shot it at the same time, one of us shot it wide with the habitat as you see in the First encounters chapter, the other shot it with their longest lens with the intention to crop it as you see here. Cropping is sometimes necessary for creative reasons, also because you don't have a big enough lens to get the reach you need (this would have needed a 1200mm+ lens). Of course you can attach a teleconverter but this loses stops of valuable light, resulting in an increase in ISO to compensate which may degrade the quality of the final image. Therefore it's essential to get the image razor sharp and with good depth of field (hence it was shot at f11), as the software interpolation process in Photoshop will pull the pixels apart. If the image is not 100% razor sharp then it will not take cropping, the usual reason for this is lack of decent shutter speed, so bear this in mind.

This famous image was shot at ISO 3200 with a 600mm and 2x teleconverter hand-held at 1/125th second. It breaks every rule; that ISO 3200 is bad quality, that you need 1/1200th second shutter speed to shoot with such a lens combination and... the list goes on. We ignored it and shot, as the moment was just too special to miss, just ignore other people's rules and shoot from your heart.

Dicky on Andy

Andy on Dicky

"I first met Andy Rouse, over a decade ago, when he came down to Ranthambhore to work on his tiger book after I had promised to get him some amazing tiger images. I had heard of Andy from before and had been following his work for a few years. I knew he was good, really good at his work. I had been living on the outskirts of Ranthambhore for over a decade and had worked with many cinematographers and photographers, though none of them was like Mr Rouse. At that time, I knew Ranthambhore better than most people in this world and I thought I knew enough about photography not to embarrass myself. The eight weeks or so that we spent together, shooting tigers in Ranthambhore in 2008, was a big milestone in my life, a time when I found a guru and a close friend. At the end of our eight weeks together, he called me a photographer. When Andy Rouse starts calling you a "photographer" you know you have arrived. I had graduated from a "camera owner" to an "outdoor photographer." Finally I had moved from taking pictures, to making them. Since then we have personally grown really close to each other, more family than friends. Over the years, we have shot a lot of images together and partied a lot, something that both of us plan to keep doing. Andy is an amazing animal photographer, though slightly crazy and that is why we get along so damn well."

"I first met Dicky in order to work on my first Tiger book. He had written me this email out of the blue criticising my existing tiger work and saying that he could get me far better images in Ranthambhore in exchange for some photographic tuition. It was cheeky to the point of me deleting the email, but there was also something about it that made me respond, and made me take that chance over 10 years ago. Since then I've become one of the family at his home and shared so many wonderful adventures, many of which you will see in this book. I've watched as he has grown in stature as a photographer, he's always had the gift of knowing tiger behaviour but I've expanded his horizons and shown him new ways of shooting. Many of the amazing infrared images in this book are his, certainly a case of the student becoming the master. As a conservationist you will never find anyone more passionate and willing to engage in the fiery world of social media to defend his beloved Ranthambhore. On the social side he is a larger than life character with an army of close friends who I now call my own; we've shared some heavy parties together too, both at Holi festival and his legendary 50th birthday week. In conclusion, Dicky is the most trustworthy, loyal and decent friend I could wish to have, and as a photographer he is simply one of the best."

Team Tiger

Our Ranthambhore team is simply the best in the business. It's total teamwork, every picture shown here (and the thousands not selected) is a result of great photography, great guiding, great driving and looking after our clients to give them a holiday of a lifetime. On the left sitting next to Dicky is one of our duo of drivers Bhaiya, a superb guy who always gets us to the right place, at the right time.

Here you can see our happy and dedicated team of local hotel staff at the Bagh, they deserve our thanks as they are very much behind the scenes but essential to everything that we do.

Drive Team - Himmat "The Boss" Singh

Since the very start of our project Himmat Singh has been part of the driving team. His knowledge of Noor, his ability to second guess her behaviour and his incredible driving skill on narrow, rock-strewn roads is second to none. We all call him "The Boss"!

Drive Team - Rajkumar Gurjar

Working with Himmat; Rajkumar is one of Ranthambhore's finest guides. His tracking and fieldcraft is amazing; many times we have followed single, small signs to lead us to Noor well ahead of anyone else. He's wonderful with our clients too and is passionate about the wildlife of Ranthambhore.

Hotel Team

At the centre of our world are our wonderful clients and a vital part of the operation are the staff at the Ranthambhore Bagh you see here. Poonam, Dicky's wife, is the boss who makes sure all the wheels run smoothly, whilst Ramsingh Gurjar and his team provide incredible service to everyone.

Client Images

We have shared so many wonderful Noor encounters over the years with our awesome clients that we thought we would let them have some glory. Here is a small selection of their favourite images and some thoughts about what Noor means to them.

Suzie - I have seen Noor as a loving mother but also like here not afraid to show the cubs who's boss.

Milt - It was such a mesmerising stare. Bold, intense, like a Tiger's Eye crystal.

Andrew - What a privilege to be in the presence of such a magnificent animal, in a truly magical place.

Guy - A truly heart pounding experience, as the magnificent Noor fights T60 to protect both her cubs and territory.

Ann - I thought, you don't mess with HER.

Gareth - Regal, Engaging, Powerful, Stunning = Very special tigress indeed!

Vic - My adrenaline surged, for a second it felt like Noor was coming for us with explosive speed and power.

Jamie - This image summed up Noor for me as a protective parent, always alert to any threats to her three beautiful cubs.

Paul - even with a kill still she looks you in the eye.

Neil - Noor has an aura unlike any other tiger I've been in the company of, incredibly powerful she demands respect.

Yvonne - The skill, power and speed at the kill, of the enigmatic Noor, has created a lifetime memory.

Ian - Thrilled to witness the awesome power and strength of Noor, demonstrated in a basic task of survival.

Paul - We were sharing a quiet relaxed moment by a waterhole… then a twig snapped…

Giles - Noor chastising her cubs lest they forget Mum knows best.

Alison - Powerful tigress, but an amazing loving, protective mother too.

John - a moment of pure perfection and family bliss that I will never forget.

Annette - Looking into her eyes touches my heart and soul, she is stunningly beautiful and majestic yet so fragile.

Mike - Nothing is so strong as gentleness. Nothing is so gentle as real strength.

Jane - I saw an experienced and relaxed wild mother allowing her cubs to roam but watchful and without doubt capable of ferocious protection. Perfect.

First published in Great Britain 2018
by Electric Squirrel Publishing
www.andyrouse.co.uk

Copyright © Andy Rouse & Aditya Singh 2018

Andy Rouse & Aditya Singh have asserted their right to be identified as
the authors of this work in accordance with the Copyright, Designs and
Patents Act 1988.

A catalogue record for this book is available from the British Library.

ISBN 978-0-9564575-3-0

Design and production: Nick Otway
Image preparation and colour repro: Andy Rouse, Mike Moody
Printed and bound in Italy by Printer Trento S.r.l.

Follow us on Instagram:

Andy Rouse @wildmanrouse

Aditya Singh @dickysingh

Our second Queen of Ranthambhore book is almost complete and
will be published in 2019. This time we follow the life of T19 Krishna,
a fantastic tigress who for many years took over the lake zones as
her home. Daughter of Ranthambhore royalty Machali she became
universally known for her rock star offspring of Arrowhead, Lightning
and Pac-man. Packed with amazing images of her life, in a totally
different landscape from Noor, it's another must have book on a
celebrity Ranthambhore tiger.

With Thanks

Andy & Dicky would like to thank the following people for their
continued assistance with their work in Ranthambhore:

R.S. Shekhawat, Sudarshan Sharma, Y K Sahu, Mukesh Saini,
Sanjiv Sharma, Mangal Singh, Dharmendra Khandal, Balendu Singh,
Salim Ali, Dharam Singh, Shivraj Singh, Ramsiya and Cheetar.

Our superb drive team of Himmat "The Boss" Singh,
Rajkumar Gurjar, Lokesh Gurjar and Sushil "Bhaiya" Chauhan.

India's foremost tiger expert Valmik Thapar for his support for this
project and superb foreword for this book.

To all our clients who have shared our wonderful adventures and
continue to do so we say a big thank you, the experience would not
have been so amazing without your support. It's been fun!

To our superb designer Nick Otway, who has been so supportive
all the way through and our proof readers Jamie and Suzie for
correcting our "enthusiasm"!!

Andy would like to say a special thanks to Tim Harris and all @ NPL,
my Canon team of Rob, Laura, Kirstie, Frankie, Jen and Siobhan,
KLM for making my journeys to India so much fun, Margot Raggett
for her crowdfunding expertise and Anup Shah (for my tiger
inspiration). Finally he would like to say a special thanks to his
partner Suzie for her constant support, encouragement and love
during tough times and for her smile which never fades even when
faced with his latest hair brained idea!!!

Additionally Andy & Dicky would like to personally thank the
managing directors of Cobra & Kingfisher Lager, whose products
have been responsible for so many wild parties and tough hangovers!